Creating Leaders
for Tomorrow

Management Master Series

William F. Christopher
Editor in Chief

Set 4: Leadership

Burt Nanus
Leading the Way to Organization Renewal

Gabriel Hevesi
Checklist for Leaders

Karl Albrecht
Creating Leaders for Tomorrow

D. Otis Wolkins
Total Quality: A Framework for Leadership

Lawrence M. Miller
From Management to Leadership

Leonard R. Sayles
High Performance Leadership:
Creating Value in a World of Change

Creating Leaders
for Tomorrow

Karl Albrecht

PRODUCTIVITY PRESS
Portland, Oregon

Management Master Series
William F. Christopher, Editor in Chief
Copyright © 1996 by Productivity Press, Inc.

Productivity Press
P.O. Box 13390
Portland, OR 97213-0390
United States of America
Telephone: 503-235-0600
Telefax: 503-235-0909
E-mail: service@ppress.com

Book design by William Stanton
Cover illustration by Paul Zwolak
Page design, graphics, and composition by Rohani Design, Edmonds, Washington
Printed and bound by BookCrafters in the United States of America

Library of Congress Cataloging-in-Publication Data

Albrecht, Karl.
    Creating leaders for tomorrow / Karl Albrecht.
      p.   cm. — (Management master series. Set 4, Leadership)
    Includes bibliographic references (p. 55).
    ISBN 1-56327-153-2. — ISBN 1-56327-101-X (pbk.)
    1. Executives. 2. Leadership. 3. Executive ability. I. Title. II. Series.
  HD38. 2.A557   1995
  658.4' 092—dc20   95-40108
                                                                   CIP

00 99 98 97 96 95 10 9 8 7 6 5 4 3 2 1

—CONTENTS—

PUBLISHER'S MESSAGE

The *Management Master Series* was designed to discover and disseminate to you the world's best concepts, principles, and current practices in excellent management. We present this information in a concise and easy-to-use format to provide you with the tools and techniques you need to stay abreast of this rapidly accelerating world of ideas.

World class competitiveness requires managers today to be thoroughly informed about how and what other internationally successful managers are doing. What works? What doesn't? and Why?

Management is often considered a "neglected art." It is not possible to know how to manage before you are made a manager. But once you become a manager you are expected to know how to manage and to do it well, right from the start.

One result of this neglect in management training has been managers who rely on control rather than creativity. Certainly, managers in this century have shown a distinct neglect of workers as creative human beings. The idea that employees are an organization's most valuable asset is still very new. How managers can inspire and direct the creativity and intelligence of everyone involved in the work of an organization has only begun to emerge.

Perhaps if we consider management as a "science" the task of learning how to manage well will be easier. A scientist begins with an hypothesis and then runs experiments to observe whether the hypothesis is correct. Scientists depend on detailed notes about the experiment—the timing, the ingredients, the amounts—and carefully record all results as they test new hypotheses. Certain things come to be known by this method; for instance, that water always consists of one part oxygen and two parts hydrogen.

We as managers must learn from our experience and from the experience of others. The scientific approach provides a model for learning. Science begins with vision and desired outcomes, and achieves its purpose through observation, experiment, and analysis of precisely recorded results. And then what is newly discovered is shared so that each person's research will build on the work of others.

Our organizations, however, rarely provide the time for learning or experimentation. As a manager, you need information from those who have already experimented and learned and recorded their results. You need it in brief, clear, and detailed form so that you can apply it immediately.

It is our purpose to help you confront the difficult task of managing in these turbulent times. As the shape of leadership changes, the *Management Master Series* will continue to bring you the best learning available to support your own increasing artistry in the evolving science of management.

We at Productivity Press are grateful to William F. Christopher and our staff of editors who have searched out those masters with the knowledge, experience, and ability to write concisely and completely on excellence in management practice. We wish also to thank the individual volume authors; Diane Asay, project manager; Julie Zinkus, manuscript editor; Karen Jones, managing editor; Lisa Hoberg and Mary Junewick, editorial support; Bill Stanton, design and production management; Susan Swanson, production coordination; Rohani Design, graphics, page design, and composition.

Norman Bodek
Publisher

1

THE NEED FOR
LEADERSHIP AT ALL LEVELS

OUR TURBULENT WORLD

All over the world, societies are changing as a result of leadership. In the last decade, the most remarkable things have been happening, not only in the developed countries, but also in so-called "third-world" countries. The human struggle for freedom, dignity, and a better life is ultimately unstoppable.

Every society and every social or business group must face and overcome obstacles in its quest for success. Progress comes from focused human energy, and it takes leadership to focus that energy.

Our societies need leadership, at many levels, more than ever before. As the populations and lifestyles of countries like the United States and others become ever more diversified, there are more issues, more problems, and more challenges to think about and act on than ever before. Life is no longer simple, and we can't just hope that "things will work themselves out" any more.

We are challenged to become less passive, more involved in the things that mean the most to our way of life, and more willing to provide leadership as individuals.

Too many people assume that their governments will take care of the major problems and important issues of their societies. This assumption is becoming less and less workable. Many of the critical issues and questions of human value facing societies today are exactly the kinds of issues governments are least equipped to handle.

A few people who have a clear vision of what they want to accomplish can shape events in remarkable ways. The events of the twentieth century have been shaped very much by the actions of committed people supported by strong leaders.

Consider the collapse of communist regimes all around the world, falling under the onslaught of *people power*. Countries like West Germany, Hungary, Poland, Czechoslovakia, Romania, Yugoslavia, and the Baltic republics have experienced mind-boggling changes in a short space of time. The USSR, once the world's showcase model of communism, virtually disintegrated under the pressure of people power.

One person can indeed make a difference. Millions of people watched their televisions sets in 1989 when a young Chinese man jumped in front of an army tank in Tian An Men Square, in the heart of Beijing and, for a brief moment at least, faced down the forces of oppression.

Individuals have always been more effective than bureaucracies at the art of moving people. And many of them have profoundly influenced their societies without having any formal authority at all.

LEADERS: BORN AND MADE

I believe it was the distinguished historian, Will Durant, who said:

> *Some men are born great, some become great, and some have greatness thrust upon them.*

The age-old question, "Are good leaders born or made?" will probably never be answered. Clearly, some people take to leadership roles with ease and grace while others struggle and flounder. Some people learn quickly, developing and maturing as leaders constantly. Some never seem to get it at all. And many more only learn to survive in leadership roles, but never become outstanding.

Some leadership theorists claim there is little point in trying to develop people as leaders, or to teach them to change their ways of leadership. They recommend merely selecting those people who have already demonstrated leadership skills and putting them into the jobs. This "leader match" theory suggests that people can't or won't learn leadership skills very well.

The "born-or-made" debate is academic. Most organizations don't have the luxury of picking outstanding, ready-made leaders. There just aren't enough to go around. Yet every organization needs a ready supply of qualified people who can move into supervisory and management jobs or take on important projects and missions. So there is no real choice but to create our own leaders. Investing in leadership development is becoming an essential part of business operations.

Of course, it makes sense to identify people who already have key leadership skills and allow them to grow into responsible jobs. It is also important to help people out of management jobs when it is clear that they are failing, if they can't grow into the jobs. It's a two-way road—selection and deselection.

WHEN LEADERS FAIL

A management or supervisory position is one of the most precious resources in an organization, and not to be squandered thoughtlessly. In any large organization, and many smaller ones, there are managers who simply can't handle their jobs. Typically, 5 to 10 percent of managers in an organization are either failing in their roles or struggling and not likely to succeed. Yet seldom does an executive team take action to develop or reassign them.

When senior executives allow a failing manager to remain in his or her situation, they do damage in a number of ways:

- The department functions ineffectively.
- Other departments may suffer as a result.
- Employees are rendered ineffective in their jobs.
- Employee morale suffers and talented people may leave.

Particularly when a failing manager is oppressive, critical, or abusive, the people in the group suffer personal stress and alienation. The hidden cost of failing management, in human and economic terms, can be enormous. Employees tend to believe that upper management knows the manager is ineffective (which is often true) and simply chooses to do nothing about it (also often true). Many of them start looking for other jobs, feeling that the situation will never change.

Many executives find it distasteful to deal with failed managers and other so-called "problem employees." They prefer to avoid it, for a number of reasons:

- a long history of tolerance for failure
- the prospect of embarrassment and hard feelings
- having to admit making a mistake in selecting the manager

Having lived with the ineffective manager for so long, they feel it's no longer possible or feasible to make a change. But a failed or failing manager is a major management problem. Senior management has a responsibility to provide all employees with competent leadership throughout the organization.

Any successful leadership development program must face and solve the problem of failing managers in order to capitalize on the prospects for developing those who can be effective.

2

HOW TO CREATE LEADERS

WHY LEADERSHIP TRAINING OFTEN FAILS

The most widely used approach for leadership development is simply a leadership training program. However, the success of leadership training over the past several decades leaves much to be desired. Many companies have invested great sums in ambitious training programs with disappointing results. Some have even created leadership "colleges" and residential programs. Most of these are hard-pressed to prove their value.

Techniques for training leaders range from the basic to the bizarre. Over the past few decades approaches have included:

- simple classroom teaching and discussion
- case studies
- sensitivity or "encounter" training
- role-playing and structured group dynamics
- team training
- coaching and mentoring
- outdoor adventure experiences

All of these methods have something to offer. Yet the track record of leadership training remains disappointing. During a seminar for the frontline employees of a large utility company, I asked how many of them had bosses who had been through the company's extensive leadership training program. Over half of them didn't know. Of those who knew, only half had noticed any difference in the way their bosses managed. The company had invested very heavily in the training program, but the results didn't show.

Many leadership training programs suffer from the same handicap: lack of transfer to real life. Managers can sit in seminars and listen, talk, role-play, do case studies, and play games. But when they go back into their leadership roles, do they use anything they've learned?

This is a common complaint with the more dramatic techniques such as encounter groups and outdoor adventure courses. Managers can paddle canoes, climb trees, rappel down the sides of cliffs, and ride rafts down raging rivers. Do any of those experiences translate into the situations they face in business?

A growing body of evidence points clearly to one missing ingredient that can make a huge difference in leadership development: feedback.

THE MAGIC POWER OF FEEDBACK

We know that feedback is an important factor in all human learning. But many training programs neglect it or omit it altogether. The only way to improve your tennis serve is to know when you've served the ball better than you did before. The only way to improve your public speaking skills is to have people tell you honestly how well you present yourself.

The famous University of California (UCLA) basketball coach John Wooden was widely considered a gifted teacher. Many sportswriters, competing coaches, and even behavioral scientists studied his methods of working with young men in a competitive-sport setting. To him, the job of coaching was one of constant feedback and development. This attitude, coupled with his uncompromisingly high expectations of his players, gave UCLA one of the outstanding basketball teams in the history of the sport.

To learn a complex set of skills like leadership, you have to have opportunities to try them out. It's one thing to hear and think about delegating. It's quite another to try it and see how it works. Without knowing how well you delegate, you can't decide to do it better.

We now understand that feedback is an essential element of the learning process, particularly with leadership skills. More and more organizations are using "360-degree" feedback systems to give managers valid, criterion-referenced feedback on their progress in learning to lead. This involves getting input from the employees in the department as well as the boss, and in some cases also from peers. Combined with the manager's own self-ratings, this information can be an important part of a development plan.[1]

ACTION LEARNING: DOING AND BECOMING

A very old Chinese expression says:

> *I hear and I forget.*
> *I see and I remember.*
> *I do and I understand.*

John Dewey, the renowned American educational theorist, said it even more simply: "People learn what they do."

Action learning is a process of learning by doing, supported by a range of other learning methods. It involves:

- getting a new idea or a new insight
- turning it into a form of action
- taking the action
- getting feedback or evaluation on how well it worked.

Only when you have had a chance to evaluate the results of your newfound skill or technique can you be sure you've learned something useful.

Action learning mirrors the natural way adults learn. As children we're conditioned to absorb information somebody else thinks is important. But as grown-ups we usually take responsibility for what we choose to learn. Adult learning usually follows a pattern:

- It tends to be project-oriented, or focused on a purpose
- It is selective; you learn what you deem most valuable
- It is multimodal; ideas come from many sources
- It is integrative; you assemble knowledge in your own way

Action learning is a powerful process for building leadership skills, because it puts the learner in charge while making use of valuable external information and the perspectives of others. It should be the main channel of effort in any leadership development program.

THE ACTION LEARNING CYCLE

Action learning is a cyclic process having three simple steps (see Figure 1):

- input
- action
- feedback

It can take place over months or even years, or it may be a matter of hours or minutes. It can apply to a large educational project or to a very simple or focused objective. Regardless of the scope or objective of the learning process, the steps are roughly the same. Think about each of these steps in relation to something you want to learn. It might be playing tennis, flying a plane, singing, using a computer, or reading financial statements.

The input step involves getting new information. You can read books, attend lectures, listen to audio or video tapes, consult with experts, swap war stories with others,

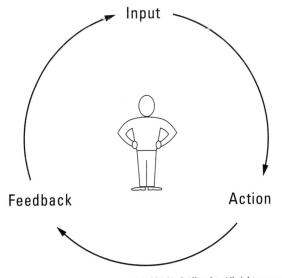

Figure 1. The Action Learning Cycle

watch skilled people in action, or do many other things to get familiar with the subject you want to learn.

The *action* step involves applying what you've found out. Hit the golf ball, speak in the foreign language, or write the mission statement for your group.

The *feedback* step involves getting a view other than your own to help you decide how well you've learned. When you speak your new foreign language to a native speaker, he or she can help you correct your pronunciation and inflection. When you discuss the mission statement you've written with your mentor or an outside consultant, he or she can give you helpful suggestions and new ideas.

The *action learning cycle* repeats itself until the learner reaches the goal, as he or she has defined it. An important part of action learning is having good sources of feedback. You can't learn much about fitness from someone who knows little about it. You can't get good advice from someone who is so opinionated he or she doesn't consider the views of others. You need to be sure the people you go to for feedback can really contribute something of value.

Some kinds of action learning involve feedback without involving people. Using a computer software package, for instance, usually involves immediate feedback. You hit a key, click the mouse, or load a file and you quickly see whether you've got the result you want. If you get stuck, you probably need input, not feedback. This is why many software products include "help" features, to give you guidance on what to do.

Each of us has a characteristic *learning style,* which is a personal preference for some methods of learning over others. Some people prefer conceptual input, and consequently are more apt to read the software manual before trying to use the system. Others learn more by doing, and prefer to jump in right away. Some people are more active and aggressive when learning something new, while others are more timid.

Because learning styles vary, there is no one correct place to start on the action learning cycle. Depending on the learning objective and a person's own learning style, any sequence of input, action, and feedback might be appropriate.

3

UNDERSTANDING LEADERSHIP

WHAT IS LEADERSHIP?

If we're going to create and develop leaders in our organizations, we first have to be sure we understand leadership as it works in the affairs of people. When we agree on what we want to develop, we can agree on ways to develop it. Let's set a framework for defining leadership.

What makes a great leader? What qualities or skills or special capabilities have the great leaders of history possessed? What made people follow them?

What makes some people successful in politics, in the military, in public life, and in corporate management, while so many others try and fail? In short, what does it take to get people to put you in charge and keep you there?

The great "movers and shakers" of history have been people who knew how to influence others. They understood people, they understood themselves, and they knew how to use the tools of authority. Not all of them were well-rounded, and not all of them were even sane. But they all knew how to be in charge. They knew how to shape the people and situations that fortune had handed them.

To answer the question of what makes a great leader we must first answer the question of what leadership really is. There are many working definitions of leadership, and probably none of them will ever be perfect. But it helps to have one as a starting point. Here is my favorite definition.

Leadership is the ability to focus human energy to achieve defined outcomes.

FORMAL AUTHORITY AND EARNED AUTHORITY

Leadership involves authority. But there is more than one kind of authority. There are actually two kinds of authority you can use in accomplishing things through people:

Formal authority is associated with your formal rank within an organization—what you are "legally" entitled to do: the ability to make decisions, allocate resources, hire, fire, promote, demote, reward, discipline, and tell people what to do.

Earned authority is the authority you as an individual have in the eyes, hearts, and minds of the people who look to you for leadership. This earned authority comes only through the personal relationships you are able to build with them, which makes them see you as someone who can help them achieve what they want in their lives.

The ideal way to influence events, of course, is to have both formal authority and earned authority in good measure. However, if you have little or no formal authority you can still be very effective if you have high earned authority. In fact, in some situations a person with no formal authority and high earned authority may have greater influence with others than another person who has high formal authority but little or no earned authority in their eyes. We all know executives, managers, or supervisors who have failed to earn the respect, trust, and allegiance of those who work for them.

Earned authority depends solely on you as a person and your ability to win people to your cause. Although an organization or a government can "issue" you a measure of formal authority, or rank, it cannot help you earn authority with others. That you must do on your own. Formal authority is a part of your formal organizational role, while earned authority is a part of the personal relationship between you and others.

THE NEW IMPERATIVE: SERVICE LEADERSHIP

One of the Latin titles used to refer to the Pope is *servus servorum,* which means "the servant of servants." This point of view suggests that anyone in a leadership role, whether it involves formal authority or not, should lead by enabling others, not by trying to drive them.

In today's world, leaders are being called upon to provide a new kind of leadership: *service leadership.* Gone are the days when a simple "command-and-control" pattern worked. The old military style of the "kick-in-the-rear" has outlived its time. It no longer fits contemporary social values, and it is no longer very effective. People in complex working situations need and expect positive personal relationships with their leaders. They want relationships that help them focus their energies, work at their best, surpass their expectations of themselves, and feel a sense of satisfaction in what they've contributed.

What is service leadership? It is the capacity to lead with a service focus:

- service to the customer
- service to the organization
- service to the employees

It means working with a spirit and a set of values that emphasize contributing something worthwhile. It means that the leader sees his or her role as enabling or helping others to accomplish something worthy, not just being in charge.

This new servant leader is willing to put empowerment above personal power; contribution above his or her own ego satisfaction; and the needs of the team above his or her own needs for credit and acclaim.

There is no higher religion than serving others.

—Albert Schweitzer

Management consultant and author Peter Block advances the case for *stewardship* as a defining motif of service leadership in the new age. According to Block:

> *Stewardship means to hold in trust the well-being of some larger entity—our organization, our community, the earth itself. This ...calls for placing service ahead of control, to no longer expect leaders to be in charge and out in front. Service is central to stewardship.*
>
> *We serve when we build capability in others by supporting ownership and choice at every level. When we act to create compliance in others, we are choosing self-interest over service, no matter what words we use to describe our actions. Service-givers who maintain dominance, aren't. Stewardship enables the use of power with grace.*[2]

The attitudes of the servant leader are very different from those traditionally inculcated into managers, particularly male managers. The "testosterone factor" typically conditions males to think in terms of authority, control, and compliance rather than in terms of ownership, empowerment, and enablement. It seems clear, however, that more and more managers, both male and female, are moving toward a broader and more versatile view of their roles, and are finding it comfortable to think in terms of leadership as a service.

Scandinavian Airlines' former chief executive Jan Carlzon even goes so far as to talk about "management by love." Paraphrasing his view:

> *Most authoritarian organizations tend to manage by fear, at least in the sense of imposing rules and punishing those who violate them. I don't believe any organization can rise above the level of mediocrity by maintaining a culture of fear. When people know they are secure in their roles, that they have someone they can turn to for help and guidance, and that their leaders believe in them, they are much more likely to go beyond the bounds of the ordinary, take risks, and contribute more of their energies and talents to the success of the organization. I call this 'management by love.'*

CUSTOMER-FOCUSED LEADERSHIP: THE SERVICE TRIANGLE

In the book *Service America!: Doing Business in the New Economy,*[3] Ron Zemke and I presented the "service triangle," shown in Figure 2. It is a pictorial model intended to show the importance of aligning the organization's *strategy, people,* and *systems* around the needs of its customers.

People in business who are trying to focus their organizations on quality are rapidly coming to the realization that *customer focus* must be the keystone of any effort to improve the organization's way of doing things. Isolated quality programs that measure and count things for the sake of measuring and counting are going out of style fast. This is why the *customer* goes at the center of the service triangle.

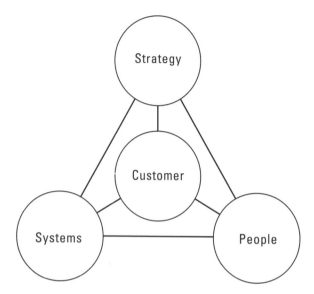

© 1984 Karl Albrecht. Used with permission.

Figure 2. The Service Triangle

Business people are also beginning to realize that, to be successful, any organization-wide focus on quality must be driven by the basic demands of the *business strategy.* What do we want to be, and how do we intend to do business? If the vision, mission, core values, and key competitive concept of the organization are not clear, any quality program will suffer from lack of focus and direction. This is why the element of *strategy* goes at the top of the service triangle.

Another important lesson of the traditional manufacturing-style approach to quality is that the effort needs to have an element of "heart" if it is to succeed. Too many quality efforts are administrative, analytical, mechanistic, control-oriented, and dehumanized. Standards-based management attempts to tighten up the organization, rather than loosen it up, and empower the people to make their own individual quality commitments. This is why the *people* are fundamental to, not an obstacle in, the service triangle.

And the all-important *systems* go into the service triangle because they are the means for achieving the ends of superior customer value. All of the methods, procedures, equipment, machinery, tools, facilities, work processes, distribution systems, organizational structures, and information systems must work toward the ultimate purpose of creating or adding value—either for the external customers or for the internal customers who depend on support departments to achieve their missions.

All three of these components of quality impinge upon the customer's experience and lead him or her to form a judgment of the value we provide at the all-important "moments of truth."

It is becoming obvious that the traditional distinction between so-called "manufacturing" organizations and "service" organizations is now obsolete, and eventually may exist only in the minds of economists. In fact, all businesses have similar issues when it comes to quality. The only difference is in the relative balance of tangible value and intangible value they respectively deliver.

As more and more executives come to understand the importance of a strategy-based, customer-value-centered approach to the success of their organizations, they are less confused by arbitrary distinctions such as "product," "quality," and "service." They begin to understand that the real issue is neither quality nor service, but *superior customer value.* And their job is to help the people of the organization create and deliver that value. The best way they can make their own contribution is by using their leadership abilities to align the *strategy, people,* and *systems* around the needs of their customers.

4

THE SIX DIMENSIONS
OF SERVICE LEADERSHIP

An effective leader is one who is highly effective in six major dimensions of accomplishment in working with others:

- Vision and Values
- Direction
- Persuasion
- Support
- Development
- Appreciation

Figure 3 shows the six components of service leadership in visual form.

As with definitions, there are many models for leadership. None is perfect, but many are workable. It is less important which model you prefer than that you choose one and exploit its most useful features. The service leadership model is one of many. I've found it helpful in a number of ways, so I've used it here.

VISION AND VALUES

To be a good visionary you have to be able to see the big picture, understand what's happening, and decide

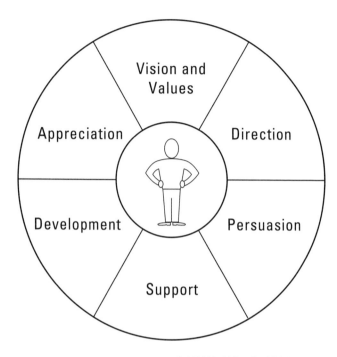

Figure 3. The Service Leadership Wheel

where your unit needs to go. You are the one who will provide the vision, spell out the purpose and contribution of your group's existence, and develop a strategy for accomplishing it. You must also take a personal stand for the values that lie behind the vision. You must know who you are, what you stand for, and what you believe to be right. And you must make these values real and compelling for others.

> *If you don't know where you want to go, any road will take you there.*

—Anon.

DIRECTION

Your job as a leader is to help people get things done. You make the strategic vision into a reality. A leader sets the overall direction for the team. This means choosing what's most important for the group to accomplish, setting goals to accomplish it, setting priorities that keep everyone's mind on the goals on a day-to-day basis, and helping everyone understand the plan.

A leader's job is to turn great thoughts into crude deeds.

—Peter Drucker

PERSUASION

It's not enough to have a clear vision and a sense of direction, although those are critical elements of effective leadership. You must also be able to get others to see, understand, and believe in the vision. As an effective leader you use your formal authority effectively—not heavy-handedly, but not in a shy way either. You are comfortably and effectively in charge. You project self-confidence in dealing with others. As a leader you can communicate clearly and with impact.

Being an effective leader means knowing how to "enroll" others in your vision.

—Warren Bennis

SUPPORT

You are there to help when people need you. You help them keep their minds focused on the real priorities, and maintain a positive frame of mind about their work. You make sure the unit operates well as a team, has the necessary resources to accomplish its mission, and has effective systems and methods to work productively. A critical part of your role as a supporter is to make effective decisions. You need to have the skills to think logically and analytically. You need a good command of essential facts and figures. And you must be able to approach problems systematically as well as creatively.

As a leader, you create a climate in your team that fosters innovation and creativity. You make sure the people know they are authorized to think. You want them to look for better ways to get things done. In your support role, your job is to organize people so well that they all know where they fit and what they have to do. You put the right people into the right roles and help them work synergistically.

Great ideas need landing gear as well as wings.

—Anon.

DEVELOPMENT

You must help people develop their capabilities and express their potential, both individually and collectively. People don't thrive as individuals when they're stuck in dead-end jobs, doing the same old things over and over. Everyone needs to be challenged at times, to take on new things, and to learn new skills. An effective leader is one who sees to it that people have a chance to grow. You have an idea of each person's skills and capabilities, his or her developmental needs, and especially his or her desires for learning and personal advancement. You occasionally discuss each person's needs and desires with them on a personal, private basis, to understand what you need to do to help them develop.

One of the most important things you need to do as a leader is expect high performance from every person on the team. Some people are better at some things than others, and others have more experience in some areas, but you should expect everyone to work effectively and make a contribution.

Man's mind, once stretched by a new idea, never returns to its original dimensions.

—Oliver Wendell Holmes

APPRECIATION

Let people know you care for and care about them. As a leader, you have a special relationship with those you lead. Once they accept you as the person to whom they will look for guidance and support in their efforts, they want to know that you recognize their work, and they want you to acknowledge their achievements. That's part of your role. A good leader can inspire people and help them feel good about what they're doing. Keep in mind the following thought.

The deepest craving in all human beings is the need to be appreciated.

—William James

All of us want respect and recognition, no matter how sophisticated we are, how educated we are, or how mature we are. Appreciation is the basic nourishment of the human soul. Good leaders know that and act on it every day.

Consider this:

> *Great leaders capture our loyalty, not by the way*
> *they make us feel about them, but by the way they*
> *make us feel about ourselves.*

> —Karl Albrecht

They help us surpass ourselves, and then they help us feel good about what we've accomplished.

LEADERSHIP AT ALL LEVELS

Leaders at all levels of the organization need to be comfortable with all six of these dimensions. Of course, each of the six will come into play in a particular form, depending on the level involved. At the senior management level, Vision and Values tend to be critically important. So are Direction and Persuasion. The other dimensions are also important, of course, but in different ways.

Moving downward through the hierarchy, we need a shift toward the operational focus. At middle levels, interpreting the Vision and Values and the Direction become important. Support is often critically important because middle managers often have to coordinate, harmonize, and reconcile the interests of various groups that have to work across organizational boundaries.

At the frontline level, tactical leaders usually have to focus much more closely on getting the actual work done. The dimensions of Support, Development, and Appreciation become critically important. They also have to understand and interpret the Vision and Values and the Direction for the people of their groups, but most of their energy usually needs to go into the practical doing of the work.

Of course, the six dimensions of the service leadership model apply equally well in situations where the leader or would-be leader has no formal managerial authority. Toastmasters International, the worldwide organization founded to develop speaking skills, has recently implemented a leadership development program available to its 8,000 local clubs.

The "High Performance Leadership" program uses an action learning design, as described previously, in which club members take on leadership challenges of their choosing. These may involve community activism, public service, business situations, or club projects. They work with self-study materials and present their results to a guidance committee for feedback. At the completion of the project, each participating member presents a speech before the club, sharing his or her learning experiences.

Executive Director Terry McCann says "Toastmasters has always emphasized public speaking skills for our members. But we've felt for some time that we needed to provide more leadership development programs as well. The action learning model is the basis for all of our programs."[4]

5

LEADERSHIP AT THE TOP

THE MAGIC POWER OF MEANING

In many ways the crisis in business today is a crisis of meaning. People aren't sure of themselves because they no longer understand the *why* behind the *what.* They no longer have the sense that things are well-defined and that hard work will lead to success. More and more people are doubtful and uncertain about the future of their organizations, and consequently, about their own careers and futures. More and more organizations and their people are in a crisis of meaning.

The late W. Edwards Deming, internationally respected quality theorist, often referred to the need for leadership in quality development. According to Deming, "a leader must have a theory. He must have a solution in mind for the problems of the organization." He was correct. I call it "knowing the way out of the woods."

In many ways, the crisis of meaning for business organizations also mirrors a crisis of meaning for nations, which is confronting people in many countries. Visit any of the major developed countries in the world and chances are you'll find an unprecedented preoccupation with questions of national purpose, cultural values, and priorities. Leaders of these nations are beset on all sides by contradictory pressures, extremist agendas, and demands for solutions. They are asking themselves: Who are we as a nation? What do we stand for? and What should be our focus and our priorities now?

And at a personal level, more and more people seem to be experiencing a parallel or derivative sense of uncertainty. Social and moral values are under debate. Social activism is on the rise; some issues are so divisive as to create intense animosity and even violence. Many people seem more focused on what divides them than on what they have in common. There is a profound need for a sense of common purpose, a commitment to a common cause.

Those who aspire to leadership roles in this new environment must not underestimate the depth of this human need for meaning. It is a most fundamental human craving, an appetite that will not go away. In his book *Man's Search for Meaning,*[5] psychologist Victor Frankl expressed the view that all human beings need a defining purpose for their lives, something to believe in, something to hope for, something to strive for. Those who lose it or never acquire it become dysfunctional at best and, in some cases, criminally maladjusted at worst.

Frankl described his experiences in the Nazi concentration camps during the second war, in which he saw prisoners who he believed simply gave up and decided to die. Living under the harshest and most brutal conditions imaginable, those who had no higher purpose in life to cling to could not hold up under the stress. Those who, like himself, believed they would eventually return to something better after the camp experience was over, were usually able to survive, at least psychologically.

Frankl named his therapeutic method *logotherapy,* after the Greek *logos,* which equates to the concept of "meaning." A *logotype,* or *logo,* is a graphic symbol used by an enterprise to communicate its identity to others.

Used in marketing and advertising, a logo can be very effective. The best leaders use figurative logos in communicating meaning within the enterprise itself, as well as with the external world.

We need a kind of logotherapy for organizations and the people living in them today. Perhaps it becomes a kind of *logoleadership,* or leadership through meaning. We can no longer rely on the forces of our environment to supply the meaning for what we do in business. Two or three decades ago, the business environment was much more stable, slow-changing, and therefore more predictable than it is now. Chief executives mostly knew what to do, and people had much of their meaning defined for them by the flow of events around them. The old imperatives were: work hard, keep focused on doing the right things, do better each year, and grow incrementally.

The new imperatives are: rethink the basics, adapt to new ways of doing business, reinvent processes, and let go of the past. In the midst of this kind of ever-changing reality, it's no wonder that people hunger for stability, meaning, and truth in their lives. We human beings cannot function indefinitely in a state of alarm and confusion. If only for our own neurotic self-preservation, we seek order and predictability in our lives, even if we have to create it artificially. People need a meaning for what they do, and many will follow dictators, demagogues, and even maniacs to get it.

But this crisis of meaning, at least in business, is as much an opportunity as a problem. Those leaders who can offer their people a valid, meaningful success proposition, and help them understand its value for them and the contribution they can make to it, have the best chance of mobilizing their energies and channeling their commitment toward worthwhile goals.

CREATING VISION

Just as the need for meaning has never been greater in the business world than now, so has the need for strong leadership never been greater. It is no longer enough for executives to merely preside over their organizations; they must lead and guide them. And the kind of leadership now called for is also different from the past. Enterprises need high-powered thinkers at the helm now, people with strong conceptual and visionary skills. A person who can exhort people, prod them, and move them to do big things will not be successful if he or she can't figure out what the right big things are. The complex changes, issues, and problems confronting businesses now demand a high level of *visionary leadership.*

The new pattern of leadership must also be an *enabling* pattern, not a commanding one. A leader might be quite impressive in his or her ability to command respect and deference, give orders, and see that they are carried out. But the way to release and mobilize the human energy in today's complex organizations is by empowering people with ideas and information, not telling them what to do. This calls for *service leadership,* not command leadership.

Today's executive must also focus unwaveringly on the critical success factor in business, namely *customer value.* This requires personally talking to and learning from customers, encouraging others throughout the organization to do the same, and making a relentless effort to translate the customers' advice into action.

FOUR ROLES OF THE EXECUTIVE LEADER

In the new world of rapid change, uncertainty, and customer-focused competition, the executive must take

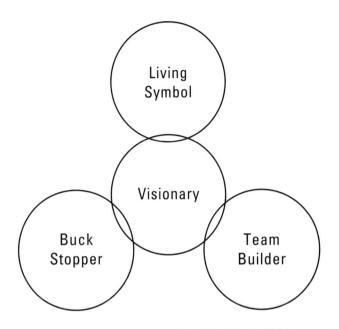

Figure 4. Four Roles of the Executive Leader

on four critical roles, or key dimensions, of his or her contribution, as illustrated in Figure 4.

- The *visionary* creates the meaning: crafts the vision, mission, and direction that define the focus of the enterprise; clarifies and distills its driving success concept; continuously evolves, elaborates, and interprets this meaning for the people of the organization.

- The *team-builder* puts the right people in the right places for the top-level leadership team, welds them into a single-minded core of advocacy for the common cause, capitalizes on their individual strengths and resources, and continuously develops them as a team and as individual leaders who can serve the mandate required of them.

- The *living symbol* "walks the talk" in a highly visible way; not necessarily by a charismatic style of leadership, but with a constant and unrelenting pattern of reinforcing the success principles of the business at every opportunity. This involves simple, everyday actions and statements as well as ceremonial and celebratory actions that enable people to associate the leader inseparably with the success premise of the enterprise. Seeing or hearing the leader automatically evokes in them powerful personal associations with the success concept. In this role the leader is, figuratively, a "human logo."

- The *buck-stopper* faces the difficult issues, discerns the truth of the challenges presented by the environment, and makes the tough decisions and dramatic changes that have to be made. This must, of course, involve open-minded listening and collaboration with the leadership team, but ultimately it is the chief executive who must face the music and manage the organization's response to critical issues.

These critical roles apply just as well to all of the executives in the leadership team as to the chief executive. Each of them must be a visionary, a team-builder, a living symbol, and a buck-stopper for his or her own enterprise within the enterprise. While allowing for natural differences in personalities and personal styles of leadership, and not expecting any one executive to be a psychological clone of the chief, nevertheless it is important that all top-level leaders face up to these same four key roles. At lower levels of the organization, tactical leaders must focus more directly on carrying out the direction, in response to the kinds of leadership they receive from the top.

People in a well-led organization tend to leave behind their old dysfunctional patterns and move toward involvement, commitment, cooperation, and a sense of shared fate. They accept and act upon the reality of their interdependence. Although even the healthiest cultures have a normal level of "politics," in a well-led enterprise the force of the vision and direction override the day-to-day frictions and collisions. People look to their leaders for answers and they look to the culture for at least some of their sense of psychological reward.

In the well-led organization there is a shared ethic of performance, a real desire to see the enterprise succeed, and a personal commitment to quality work. Whereas in the poorly-led organization people tend to move away from and against one another and their leaders, in the well-led organization they tend to move with and toward them. They see their personal success as in some way connected to the success of the enterprise.

6

LEADERSHIP IN THE MIDDLE

MANAGEMENT AND LEADERSHIP ARE NOT THE SAME

We are reaching a point in business thinking where even the concept of management is suspect, and the basic term itself is falling into disrepute. Management, in its traditional connotation, has always implied the control of the many by the few. It has signaled an autocratic, systematic, and intellectual thought process, not a human, dynamic, and personal one. Traditional "B-school thinking" has always viewed the manager as operating the organization, as if it were some kind of apparatus to be manipulated.

Dr. Warren Bennis, professor at the University of Southern California, asserts that "Today's employee is overmanaged and underled. We have too much management in our organizations today, and not enough leadership." As we move ahead into ever more turbulent times and face ever more complex and challenging problems, there simply has to be a shift of emphasis in management thinking. We must leave behind the traditional preoccupation with the organizational structure and its processes, and move toward a much more diversified thinking process that focuses on the creation of value, mobilizes collective intelligence, and projects a compelling concept of the meaning of the enterprise. And we have to learn how to enable the people of the enterprise to create unprecedented levels of value for the customer, the organization, and themselves.

MIDDLE MANAGEMENT: A NO-WIN JOB?

Middle managers may be the least understood species in the entire organizational menagerie. As a segment of working society, they have come in for more criticism, more blame, and more scorn in recent years than any other. They seem to fulfill some primitive need we have for someone to persecute for the failings of large organizations.

Pejorative terms abound for describing middle managers. Some Scandinavian executives call them "the rockwool layer," meaning that they're like a fuzzy layer of insulation between upper and lower levels of the organization, preventing ideas and information from flowing in either direction. The British call them "the damp layer," suggesting that they water down and cool down all the exciting ideas that come their way. Americans tend to call them simply "the bureaucracy."

Some organizational theorists are calling for the elimination of middle managers, almost as if by surgery. The reasoning goes: if an organ is not doing its job, cut it out. Some are predicting that the proliferation of computers and the increasingly knowledge-intensive nature of organizations will solve the problem naturally. Eventually it will be only the senior executives, the frontline workers, maybe some supervisors, and a whole bunch of computers and networks. Information and ideas will flow freely and the whole organization will be much more dynamic.

That, of course, won't happen. We do not need a way to get rid of all middle managers, because we need them, or at least many of them. We need a way to enfranchise them as leaders.

A middle-management job in many organizations, especially large ones, is a no-win deal. Middle managers often feel themselves hemmed in by policies, procedures, and rules of someone else's making, and at the same time they feel themselves under pressure to innovate, communicate, and manage change. They feel pressure from the top and demands from the bottom. They typically have less latitude for action than onlookers seem to think they have, or at least they perceive themselves as having less.

Most middle managers have "no-go power," but no "go power." They are usually in the position of approving or disapproving (no-go power), but they can seldom originate things (go power). This is typically a fact of organizational structures and the division of authority. Nothing we can say here applies to 100 percent of middle managers, of course, but it seems to be true that most of them have been created as functionaries rather than leaders.

In most organizations, probably the vast majority, middle managers slip quietly and comfortably into these passive gatekeeping roles, often with no thought at all for alternative approaches. Most of us human beings are quite malleable. Whether we like to admit it or not, most of us tend to take on the mind-sets and habit patterns of the roles in which we find ourselves. If the nature of the role suggests coordination, we become coordinators. If it suggests budgeting and resource allocation, we become budgeteers. If it suggests approving and vetoing, we learn the thumbs-up and thumbs-down responses and often little else.

Middle managers in any organization are typically reflections of the prevailing organizational culture. In a company culture that is risk-averse, rule-based, and ritualistic, they tend to become risk-averse, rule-based, and ritualistic. Bureaucracy begets bureaucracy. The style and attitudes of the chief executive often have a big influence on the habits of the middle managers. If the top person is a caretaker, you tend to get caretaker management. If he or she is a bureaucrat, you tend to get bureaucrats. There often tends to be a "cloning" effect, in which the middle-level managers project the kinds of managerial styles they believe the chief wants to see. In some cases the chief executive himself is little more than a middle manager with nobody above him.

SOLVING THE MIDDLE MANAGEMENT PROBLEM

The "middle management problem" is really a problem of role confusion, not a problem of incompetence. Therefore, the solution must come through role clarification, not through recrimination and persecution. We must understand the dilemma many middle managers find themselves in, and help them find ways out of that dilemma.

Three things have to happen for middle managers to become the kinds of service leaders needed by their organizations and their people. They need to:

- adopt a new mind-set about themselves and their roles.

- think through the roles of their organizations in the context of the goals of the overall business of which they are a part.

- have the support of a service-oriented organizational culture around and above them.

Most important is the new mind-set. The old mind-set is one of administration, procedure, approval and disapproval, and passively reacting to events and problems presented by others. The new mind-set must be a proactive one. It must be entrepreneurial in its focus. It must be broader in its scope. And it must be much more business-focused than in the past.

This will require some careful teaching and development of middle managers. Some of them operate this way already, but by no means most. Managers will have to learn this new mind-set, and that will take some impetus from the leaders above them. As more and more of them learn and adopt it, it may well become contagious. Good role models can serve to project the possibilities to others better than anything else.

Putting these three causal factors together—a new mind-set, a new plan of attack, and a reinforcing service culture—is not an easy task, by any means. But it is most definitely possible. And by breaking it down into its essential components and making it a teachable methodology, determined executives and well-intentioned middle managers can team up to bring it about.

FIVE STEPS TO MIDDLE MANAGEMENT LEADERSHIP

A middle manager who wants to move from the old role of bureaucrat to a new role of entrepreneurial leader needs to do five things:

- Define the real contribution of the department, in terms of the customers it serves, both internal and external.

- Define and articulate a clear mission for service.

- Train, develop, and orient the people of the unit for creating value, not just for doing tasks.

- Focus the systems and procedures on the delivery of service and the creation of customer value.

- Focus the rewards on service, to appreciate those who contribute to the success of the enterprise.

7

LEADERSHIP AT THE FRONT

THREE THINGS EVERY
TACTICAL LEADER MUST DO

Frontline supervisors are the tactical leaders of the organization. They have the special responsibility of turning great thoughts into crude deeds. If leadership consists of focusing human energy to achieve defined outcomes, they are the primary people who work to focus that energy. They have to get things done.

Frontline leaders need to work smart, as well as hard. They have to do three things to make their special contribution:

- understand the vision of the enterprise; the mission, the driving values, the priorities, where it's going

- keep the attention of their people focused on creating value, not just on doing tasks

- capitalize on all the brain power they have at their disposal

All three of these elements are closely connected. The job of the frontline supervisor is to translate the business direction into meaning for the people of the unit. They need to understand how the work of the unit contributes to the higher purpose. Having gotten this message across, the supervisor has to keep it in the center of their field of view all the time. And once they know what contribution is expected of them, individually and collectively, the supervisor must help them put their energy and know-how to work.

MANAGING BRAINS
AND MOBILIZING INTELLIGENCE

Every organization is blessed with an abundant supply of brain power. Yet few of them seem to take advantage of it to the extent that they easily could. The leaders of most organizations seem content to pay the costs of having people on the payroll, but pay little attention to the question of whether these "resources" are creating value. Managers who regularly upgrade capital equipment, plants, and facilities in order to make them generate more value routinely neglect and ignore one of the most expensive resources they have—the people.

In a way, all management is the management of brains. In today's organizations, fewer and fewer jobs can be done without a contribution of the worker's brain power, although many organizations still try to design jobs that way. The frontline leader has to help all of these brains, and the people who own them, to make their best contribution.

Some years ago, in a book titled *Brain Power*, I modestly proposed Albrecht's *law of collective dumbness:*[6]

> *Intelligent people, when assembled into an organization, can sometimes do dumb things collectively.*

Surely we all wonder from time to time whether it's possible for an organization to stop making the same mistakes over and over, and to use the collective knowledge, know-how, and wisdom it has. Yet we still see collective dumbness demonstrated repeatedly in everyday organizational life. It happens when people miscommunicate, fail to cooperate and collaborate, and work at cross purposes because their activities are not coordinated or harmonized. Sometimes it's comical, sometimes it's tragic. It's almost always wasteful or destructive in its effect.

There's a specially destructive version of collective dumbness, one which is profound and pernicious in its implications for organizational success or failure. It is the deliberate "dumbing down" of the workforce through traditional management techniques that have been accepted and glorified for four or five decades. While the Japanese are working hard at finding ways to leverage individual intelligence for collective good, many Western managers, academics, and management consultants are still working hard at figuring out how to exclude individual brain power from organizational processes. This is what Swedish managers refer to in American management practices as "the systematic stupification of the worker."

Imagine that a typical organization or unit has 100 employees, and that each of them has approximately the average IQ score of 100 points. Multiplying 100 IQ points by 100 people, we get a total of 10,000 IQ points. The critical question is, how many of these IQ points is our organization actually using? Bear in mind that we've already paid for them, whether we use them or not. When the employee shows up for work, we've already purchased his or her 100 or so IQ points, or at least we have an option on them. By the end of each day, we have either exercised the option or we've let it expire. That day will never come again, and the option on that day's IQ points is gone forever.

While managers in America and other Western countries are busy figuring out how to standardize workers along with everything else in the organization, the Japanese are figuring out how to exercise the option on the IQ points. Just imagine the possibilities, if we could learn how to do it. Instead of starting with 10,000 IQ points and whittling them down to a few thousand or a few hundred by robotizing and standardizing the employees, suppose we can exercise the option on all 10,000 points. Suppose we can even go further, and create synergy by inviting people to contribute their best ideas and inventions as well as their basic job knowledge. Suppose we can multiply the 10,000 IQ points a hundred-fold. We could have a collective organizational IQ of a million.

When frontline leaders understand the *support* and *development* dimensions of the service leadership model, they help people develop and mobilize their brain power for the benefit of the enterprise.

8

FINDING AND DEVELOPING TOMORROW'S LEADERS

WHAT DOES EMPOWERMENT REALLY MEAN?

There is great discussion lately of the idea of empowering employees. However, the talk is usually much more grand than the action. For many organizations and many managers, empowerment remains nothing more than a slogan. But for some, it means specific actions and practices that liberate human energy and brain power, and take advantage of individual know-how.

Empowerment is all about natural leadership. It's about challenging people and letting them meet the challenge in their own ways. It's also about challenging managers to release more and more control and to rethink their own power needs. It implies a very different way of working and getting things done than we've used in the past. Many managers will have difficulty getting comfortable with it.

Frontline leaders empower employees when they:

- communicate and dramatize the big picture, the mission of the enterprise, and the contribution of the group to it

- manage in terms of outcomes, not tasks

- assign responsibilities in terms of missions, or dimensions of contribution, not job functions

- grant employees wide latitude in deciding how to create their assigned outcomes

- guide and advise, rather than control and meddle

- maintain active communication, so employees can coordinate their efforts and approach their problems in ways that create synergy rather than conflict

HOW TO RELEASE
LEADERSHIP POTENTIAL

Not all managers are comfortable with the idea of empowered employees. And not all employees want to be empowered. Many people prefer having someone tell them just what to do, so they don't have to take personal responsibility for results. We can't expect to turn all employees into skilled leaders.

We can, however, create the conditions that will invite those with the interest and potential for leadership to grow and develop. This pays off in several ways:

- It gets things done better, because more people are proactively using their common sense and taking the initiative.

- It increases the number of people eligible for leadership jobs.

- It decreases the likelihood of putting the wrong people into leadership jobs and having to remove them later.

We can release greater leadership potential in the organization when we:

- create and maintain an atmosphere of empowerment, which encourages people to take the initiative and holds them accountable for their results

- create and maintain a *performance culture,* that is, one in which there is a healthy pressure to perform and a value system that encourages success

- create natural opportunities for people to tackle leadership roles and test themselves in action, without needing to be in formal supervisory roles

- set up training and development activities that enable people to learn leadership skills and put them to use

THE THREE GATES TO BECOMING A BOSS

There is a fairly easy way to solve the problem of the failing or failed manager, as discussed previously. All we have to do is make sure that the only people who get into leadership jobs are those qualified to handle them.

Many firms do it backwards. They appoint people to management positions for all the wrong reasons. The best accountant in the group gets appointed head of the accounting group, with no assessment of whether he or she can handle the job. The best underwriter, or design engineer, or sales person gets thrown into the department-head job, often with no assessment and little preparation.

It is wise to set up ways to prevent people from getting appointed to management jobs before they are ready. By carefully selecting leader candidates, developing them properly, and testing them for qualifications, it is possible to eliminate most of the management "flunk-out" problem.

The way to do this is to set up three figurative *gates* to getting into a management position. No person should be placed in a management job without passing three key tests:

- They actually want a management job, or at least they have declared that they want to give it a try.

- They have taken at least a basic training course in supervision, so that they know what a supervisory job is all about.

- They compete fairly for the job against their peers.

In addition, every appointment to a management job should be made on a probationary basis, to allow a graceful retreat if the person doesn't fit the needs of the position. No executive or manager should have the right to slip his or her personal protege or favored person into a leadership job without giving all qualified candidates a fair chance.

These are fairly stringent conditions. They require that senior managers and middle managers think ahead. Instead of doing nothing until a management job opens up and then looking around to see who might fit into it, the leaders of the organization need to be developing eligible people right along. Instead of just tossing the nearest candidate into the job, they need to think of the job as a valuable resource for the organization. How should it be invested? How can we make sure the person to whom we entrust that position will perform effectively?

THE PLAN FOR LEADERSHIP DEVELOPMENT

Leadership development doesn't happen by accident. An organization doesn't just accumulate a supply of effective leaders without concerted action on the part of its senior executives. Part of leadership is developing leaders.

To summarize and review, the three key components of an effective leadership development program are:

- careful selection of candidates
- training and development
- survey-guided assessment and feedback

Using the action-learning format described previously, executives and HRD departments can create a natural process that supports the development of human potential and enables the enterprise to compete effectively for the future. And the future, after all, is where the action is.

NOTES

1. One such 360-degree assessment instrument is Leadex: Leadership Assessment System, available through Karl Albrecht International, (619) 622-4884.

2. Peter Block, *Stewardship: Choosing Service Over Self-interest* (San Francisco: Berrett-Koehler, 1992).

3. Karl Albrecht and Ron Zemke, *Service America!: Doing Business in the New Economy* (Homewood, Ill.: Dow Jones-Irwin, 1985).

4. Karl Albrecht, "High Performance Leadership," proprietary self-study program of Toastmasters International. All rights reserved by Karl Albrecht. Used with permission.

5. Victor Frankl, *Man's Search for Meaning* (Boston: Beacon Press, 1992).

6. Karl Albrecht, *Brain Power: Learn to Improve Your Thinking Skills* (Engelwood Cliffs, N.J.: Prentice-Hall, 1980).

ABOUT THE AUTHOR

Karl Albrecht is a management consultant, speaker, and a prolific author. His 20 books on management, organizational effectiveness, and personal effectiveness include the bestsellers *Service America!*, *The Only Thing That Matters*, and *The Northbound Train*.

As chairman of Karl Albrecht International, he oversees the practical application of his concepts through a consulting firm (The TQS Group), a training firm (Albrecht Training & Development), and a publishing firm (Albrecht Publishing Company).

Karl Albrecht
Karl Albrecht International
4320 La Jolla Village Drive, Suite 310
San Diego, CA 92122
Phone: (619) 622-4884
Fax: (619) 622-4885

PRAISE FOR THE MANAGEMENT MASTER SERIES

"A rare information resource.... Each book is a gem; each set of six books a basic library.... Handy guides for success in the '90s and the new millennium."

Otis Wolkins
Vice President Quality Services/Marketing
Administration, GTE

"Productivity Press has provided a real service in its *Management Master Series*. These little books fill the huge gap between the 'bites' of oversimplified information found in most business magazines and the full-length books that no one has enough time to read. They have chosen very important topics in quality and found well-known authors who are willing to hold themselves within the 'one plane trip's worth' length limitation. Every serious manager should have a few of these in their reading backlog to help keep up with today's new management challenges."

C. Jackson Grayson, Jr.
Chairman, American Productivity & Quality Center

"The *Management Master Series* takes the Cliffs Notes approach to management ideas, with each monograph a tight 50 pages of remarkably meaty concepts that are defined, dissected, and contextualized for easy digestion."

Industry Week

"A concise overview of the critical success factors for today's leaders."

Quality Digest

"A wonderful collection of practical advice for managers."

Edgar R. Fiedler
Vice President and Economic Counsellor,
The Conference Board

"A great resource tool for business, government, and education."

Dr. Dennis J. Murray
President, Marist College

PRODUCTIVITY PRESS, Dept. BK, PO Box 13390, Portland, OR 97213-0390
Telephone: 1-800-394-6868   Fax: 1-800-394-6286

THE MANAGEMENT MASTER SERIES

The Management Master Series offers business managers leading-edge information on the best contemporary management practices. Written by respected authorities, each short "briefcase book" addresses a specific topic in a concise, to-the-point presentation, using both text and illustrations. These are ideal books for busy managers who want to get the whole message quickly.

Great Management Ideas

Management Alert: Don't Reform—Transform!
Michael J. Kami
Transform your corporation: adapt faster, be more productive, perform better.

Vision, Mission, Total Quality: Leadership Tools for Turbulent Times
William F. Christopher
Build your vision and mission to achieve world class goals.

The Power of Strategic Partnering
Eberhard E. Scheuing
Take advantage of the strengths in your customer-supplier chain.

New Performance Measures
Brian H. Maskell
Measure service, quality, and flexibility with methods that address your customers' needs.

Motivating Superior Performance
Saul W. Gellerman
Use these key factors—non-monetary as well as monetary—to improve employee performance.

Doing and Rewarding: Inside a High-Performance Organization
Carl G. Thor
Design systems to reward superior performance and encourage productivity.

PRODUCTIVITY PRESS, Dept. BK, PO Box 13390, Portland, OR 97213-0390
Telephone: 1-800-394-6868   Fax: 1-800-394-6286

Total Quality

The 16-Point Strategy for Productivity and Total Quality
William F. Christopher/Carl G. Thor
Essential points you need to know to improve the performance of your organization.

The TQM Paradigm: Key Ideas That Make It Work
Derm Barrett
Get a firm grasp of the world-changing ideas beyond the Total Quality movement.

Process Management: A Systems Approach to Total Quality
Eugene H. Melan
Learn how a business process orientation will clarify and streamline your organization's capabilities.

Practical Benchmarking for Mutual Improvement
Carl G. Thor
Discover a down-to-earth approach to benchmarking and building useful partnerships for quality.

Mistake-Proofing: Designing Errors Out
Richard B. Chase and Douglas M. Stewart
Learn how to eliminate errors and defects at the source with inexpensive *poka-yoke* devices and staff creativity.

Communicating, Training, and Developing for
Quality Performance
Saul W. Gellerman
Gain quick expertise in communication and employee development basics.

PRODUCTIVITY PRESS, Dept. BK, PO Box 13390, Portland, OR 97213-0390
Telephone: 1-800-394-6868   Fax: 1-800-394-6286

Customer Focus

Designing Products and Services That Customers Want
Robert King
Here are guidelines for designing customer-exciting products and services to meet the demands for continuous improvement and constant innovation to satisfy customers.

Creating Customers for Life
Eberhard E. Scheuing
Learn how to use quality function deployment to meet the demands for continuous improvement and constant innovation to satisfy customers.

Building Bridges to Customers
Gerald A. Michaelson
From the priceless value of a single customer to balancing priorities, Michaelson delivers a powerful guide for instituting a customer-based culture within any organization.

Delivering Customer Value: It's Everyone's Job
Karl Albrecht
This volume is dedicated to empowering people to deliver customer value and aligning a company's service systems.

Shared Expectations: Sustaining Customer Relationships
Wayne A. Little
How to create a process for sharing expectations and building lasting and profitable relationships with customers and suppliers that incorporates performance goals and measures.

Service Recovery: Fixing Broken Customers
Ron Zemke
Here are the guidelines for developing a customer-retaining service recovery system that can be a strategic asset in a company's total quality effort.

PRODUCTIVITY PRESS, Dept. BK, PO Box 13390, Portland, OR 97213-0390
Telephone: 1-800-394-6868   Fax: 1-800-394-6286

Leadership

Leading the Way to Organization Renewal
Burt Nanus
How to build and steer a continually renewing and transforming organization by applying a vision to action strategy.

Checklist for Leaders
Gabriel Hevesi
Learn to focus day-to-day decisions and actions, leadership, communications, team building, planning, and efficiency.

Creating Leaders for Tomorrow
Karl Albrecht
How to mobilize all the intelligence of the organization to create value for customers.

Total Quality: A Framework for Leadership
D. Otis Wolkins
Consider the problems and opportunities in today's world of changing technology, global competition, and rising customer expectations in terms of the leadership role.

From Management to Leadership
Lawrence M. Miller
A visionary analysis of the qualities required of leaders in today's business: vision and values, enthusiasm for customers, teamwork, and problem-solving skills at all levels.

High Performance Leadership: Creating Value in a World of Change
Leonard R. Sayles
Examine the need for leadership involvement in work systems and operations technology to meet the increasing demands for short development cycles and technologically complex products and services.

PRODUCTIVITY PRESS, Dept. BK, PO Box 13390, Portland, OR 97213-0390
Telephone: 1-800-394-6868   Fax: 1-800-394-6286

ABOUT PRODUCTIVITY PRESS

Productivity Press exists to support the continuous improvement of American business and industry.

Since 1983, Productivity has published more than 100 books on the world's best manufacturing methods and management strategies. Many Productivity Press titles are direct source materials translated for the first time into English from industrial leaders around the world.

The impact of the Productivity publishing program on Western industry has been profound. Leading companies in virtually every industry sector use Productivity Press books for education and training. These books ride the cutting edge of today's business trends and include books on total quality management (TQM), corporate management, Just-In-Time manufacturing process improvements, total employee involvement (TEI), profit management, product design and development, total productive maintenance (TPM), and system dynamics.

To get a copy of the full-color catalog, call 800-394-6868 or fax 800-394-6286.

To view sample chapters and see the complete line of books, visit the Productivity Press online catalog on the Internet at *http://www.ppress.com/*

Productivity Press titles are distributed to the trade by National Book Network, 800-462-6420

TO ORDER: Write, phone, or fax Productivity Press, Dept. BK, P.O. Box 13390, Portland, OR 97213-0390, phone 800-394-6868, fax 800-394-6286. Send check or charge to your credit card (American Express, Visa, MasterCard accepted).

PRODUCTIVITY PRESS, Dept. BK, PO Box 13390, Portland, OR 97213-0390
Telephone: 1-800-394-6868   Fax: 1-800-394-6286

TO ORDER: Write, phone, or fax Productivity Press, Dept. BK, P.O. Box 13390, Portland, OR 97213-0390, phone 1-800-394-6868, fax 1-800-394-6286. Send check or charge to your credit card (American Express, Visa, MasterCard accepted).

U.S. ORDERS: Add $5 shipping for first book, $2 each additional for UPS surface delivery. Add $5 for each AV program containing 1 or 2 tapes; add $12 for each AV program containing 3 or more tapes. We offer attractive quantity discounts for bulk purchases of individual titles; call for more information.

ORDER BY E-MAIL: Order 24 hours a day from anywhere in the world. Use either address:
To order: *service@ppress.com*
To view the online catalog and/or order:
  http://www.ppress.com/

QUANTITY DISCOUNTS: For information on quantity discounts, please contact our sales department.

INTERNATIONAL ORDERS: Write, phone, or fax for quote and indicate shipping method desired. For international callers, telephone number is 503-235-0600 and fax number is 503-235-0909. Prepayment in U.S. dollars must accompany your order (checks must be drawn on U.S. banks). When quote is returned with payment, your order will be shipped promptly by the method requested.

NOTE: Prices are in U.S. dollars and are subject to change without notice.